THE PHILLIP KEVEREN SERIES PIANO SOLO

QUEEN FOR CLASSICAL PIANO

Cover Photo © AF archive / Alamy Stock Photo

— PIANO LEVEL —
ADVANCED

ISBN 978-1-4950-5909-4

HAL•LEONARD®
CORPORATION

7777 W. BLUEMOUND RD. P.O. BOX 13819 MILWAUKEE, WI 53213

In Australia Contact:
Hal Leonard Australia Pty. Ltd.
4 Lentara Court
Cheltenham, Victoria, 3192 Australia
Email: ausadmin@halleonard.com.au

Visit Hal Leonard Online at
www.halleonard.com

Visit Phillip at
www.phillipkeveren.com

PREFACE

In the summer of 1976, I turned 15 years old. "Bohemian Rhapsody" was all over the radio waves. I had never heard anything like it, and I could not get enough of it! The magical merging of opera and rock made a huge impression on me.

Queen was one of the most successful rock bands in music history. With estimates of record sales ranging from 150 million to 300 million, they were inducted into the Rock and Roll Hall of Fame in 2001. Their songs took inspiration from many different genres of music. With such a rich musical palette from which to draw, arranging these gems for classical piano was extremely enjoyable.

Musically yours,

Phillip Keveren

BIOGRAPHY

Phillip Keveren, a multi-talented keyboard artist and composer, has composed original works in a variety of genres from piano solo to symphonic orchestra. Mr. Keveren gives frequent concerts and workshops for teachers and their students in the United States, Canada, Europe, and Asia. Mr. Keveren holds a B.M. in composition from California State University Northridge and a M.M. in composition from the University of Southern California.

ANOTHER ONE BITES THE DUST

Words and Music by
JOHN DEACON
Arranged by Phillip Keveren

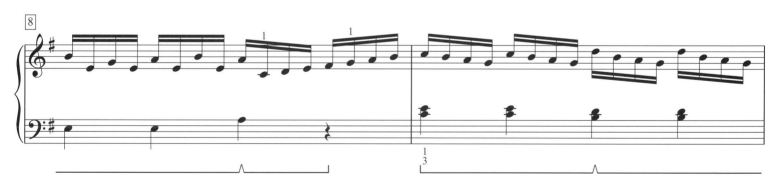

4

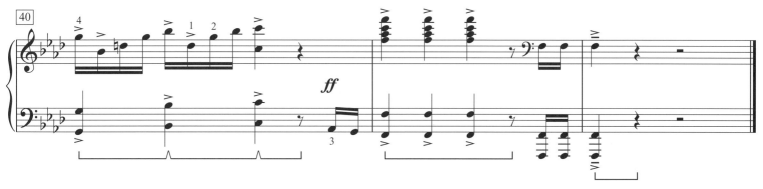

BICYCLE RACE

Words and Music by
FREDDIE MERCURY
Arranged by Phillip Keveren

8

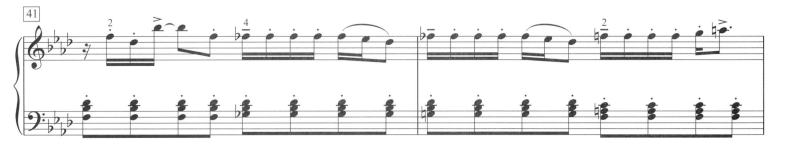

BOHEMIAN RHAPSODY

Words and Music by
FREDDIE MERCURY
Arranged by Phillip Keveren

Slowly (♩ = 69-72)

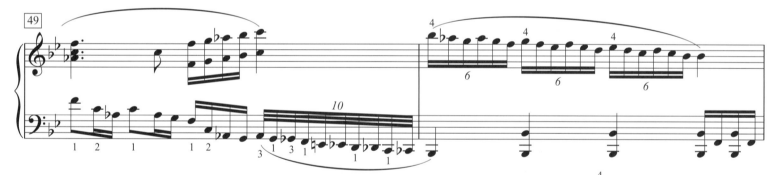

senza pedale

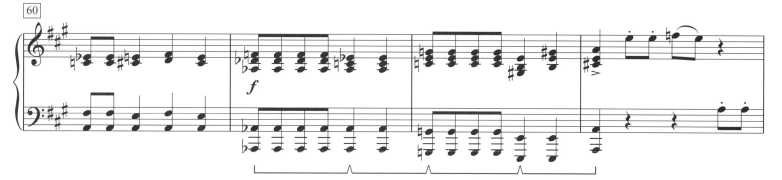

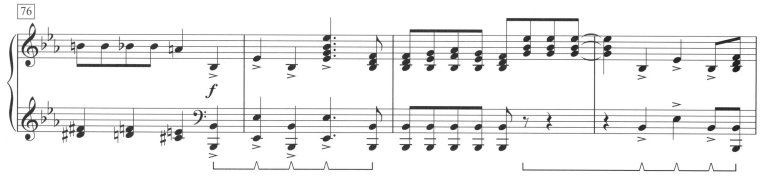

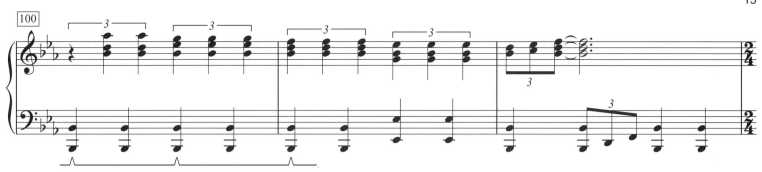

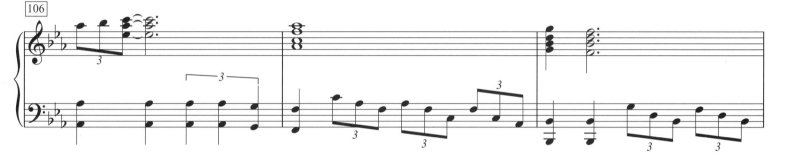

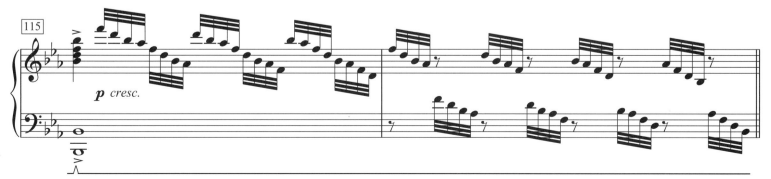

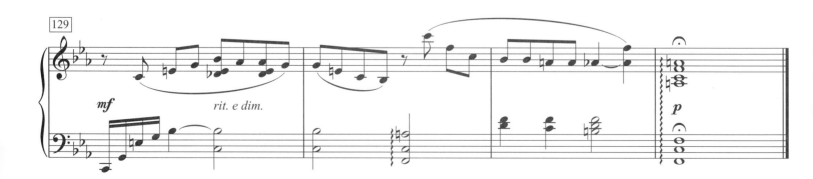

BRIGHTON ROCK

Words and Music by
BRIAN MAY
Arranged by Phillip Keveren

Allegro (♩ = 138)

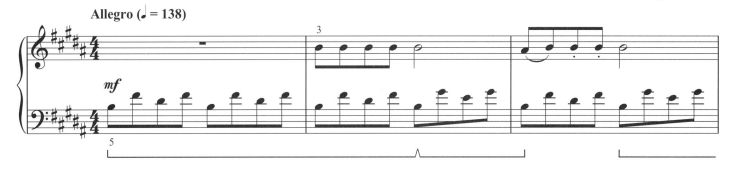

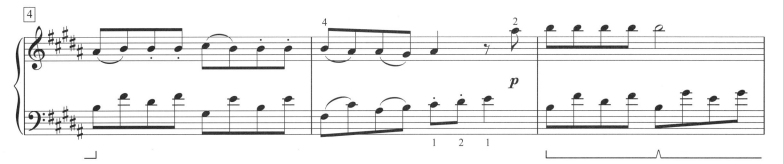

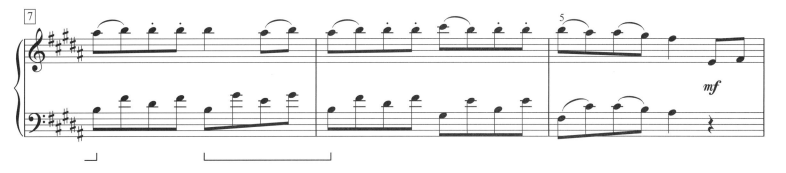

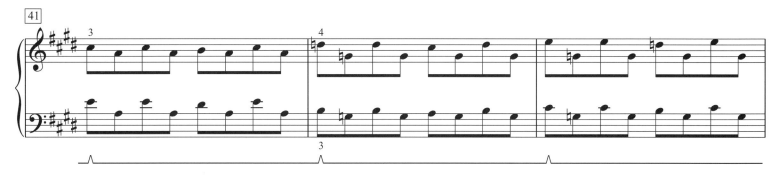

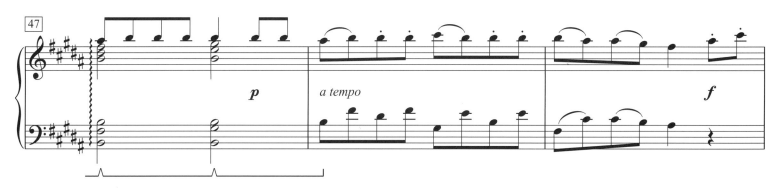

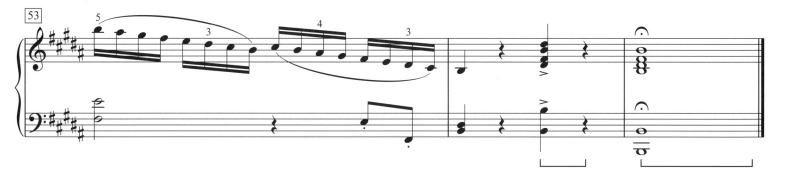

CRAZY LITTLE THING CALLED LOVE

Words and Music by
FREDDIE MERCURY
Arranged by Phillip Keveren

Vigorously (♩. = 152)

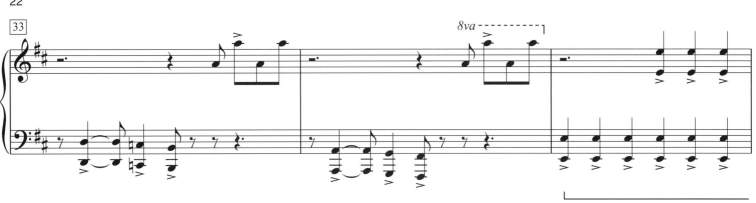

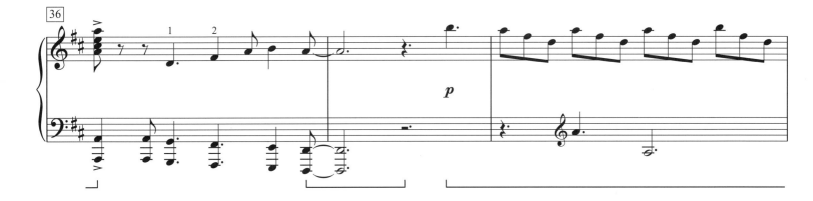

KILLER QUEEN

Words and Music by
FREDDIE MERCURY
Arranged by Phillip Keveren

With swagger (♩. = 116)

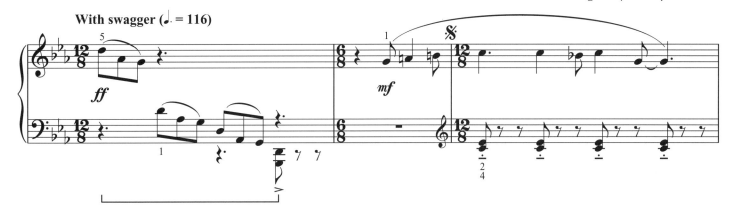

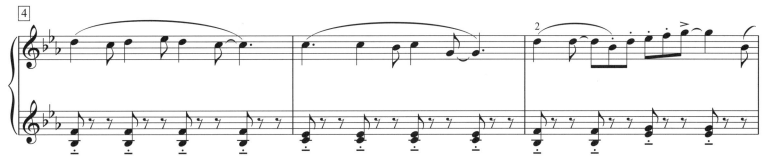

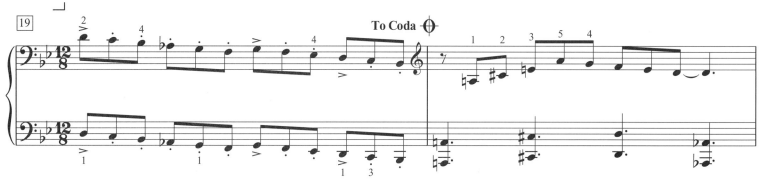

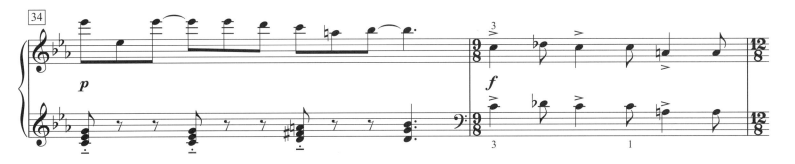

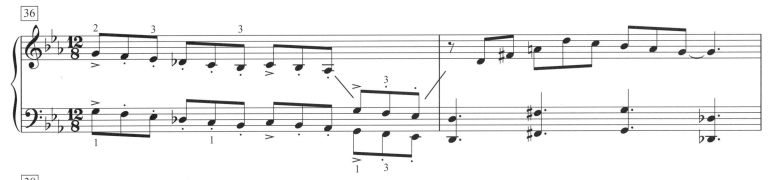

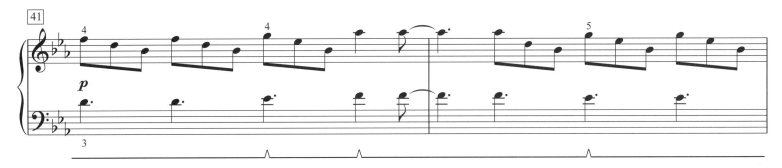

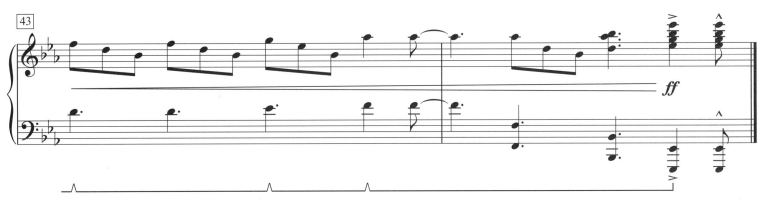

FLASH'S THEME
(Flash)

Words and Music by
BRIAN MAY
Arranged by Phillip Keveren

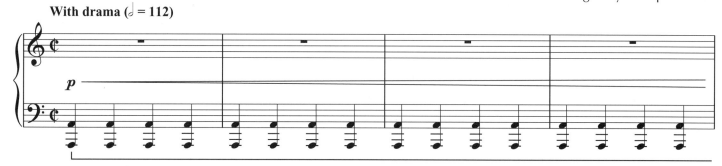

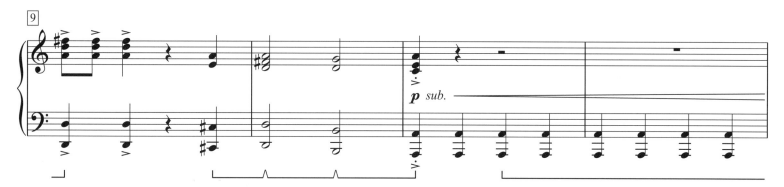

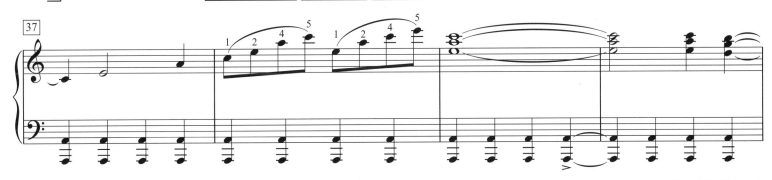

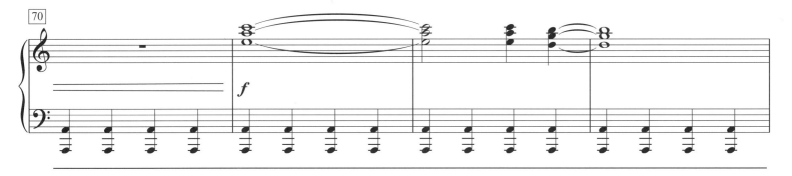

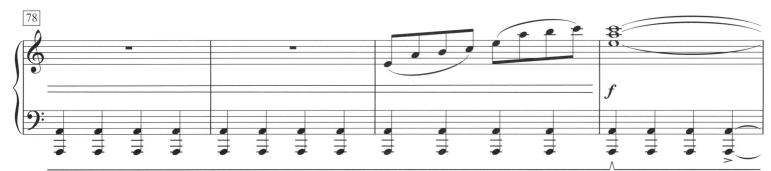

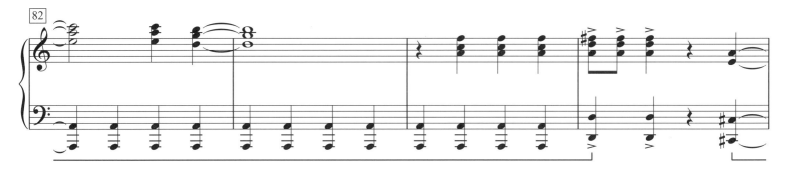

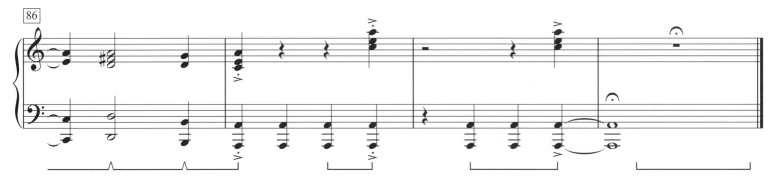

RADIO GA GA

Words and Music by
ROGER TAYLOR
Arranged by Phillip Keveren

Like a gentle breeze (♩ = 80)

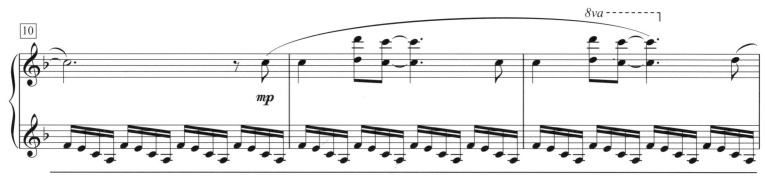

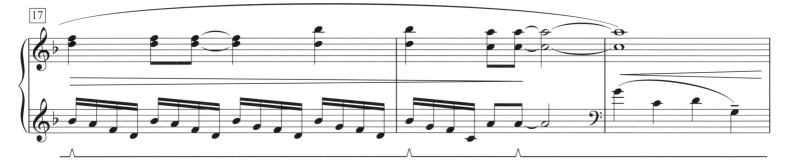

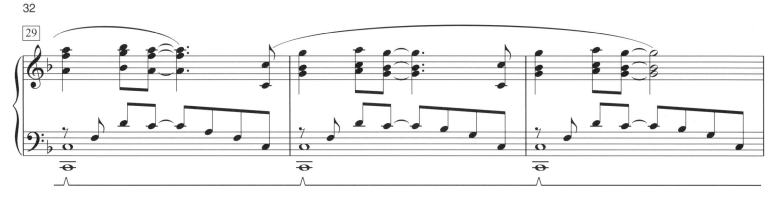

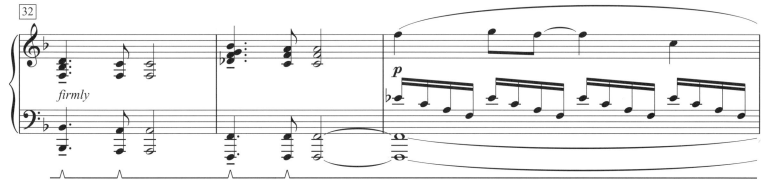

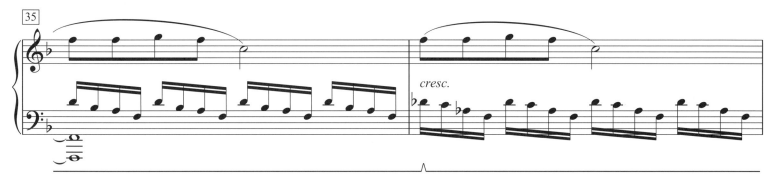

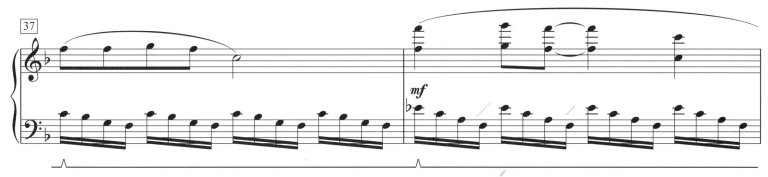

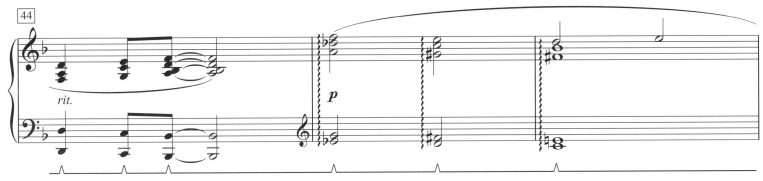

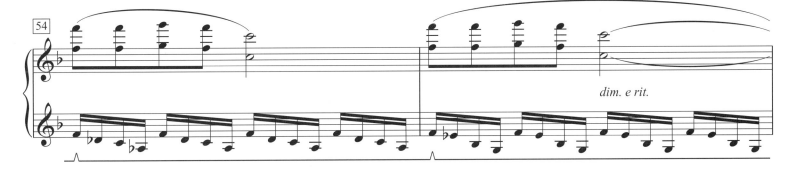

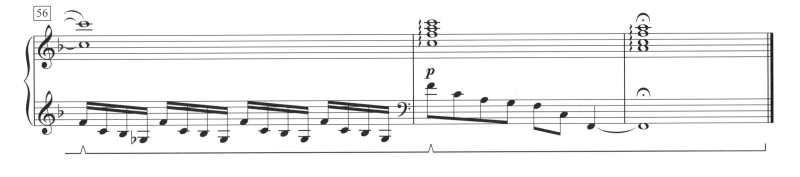

SOMEBODY TO LOVE

Words and Music by
FREDDIE MERCURY
Arranged by Phillip Keveren

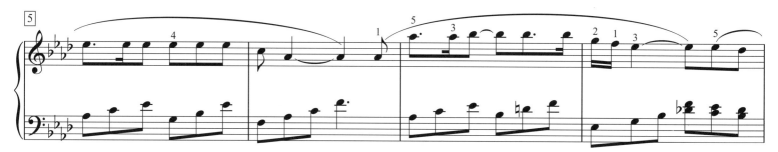

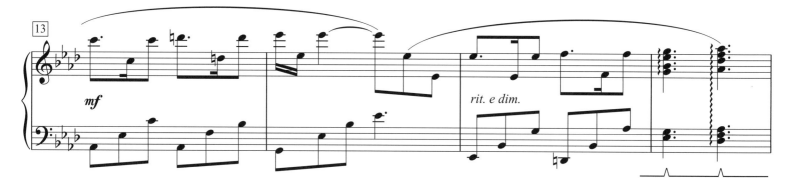

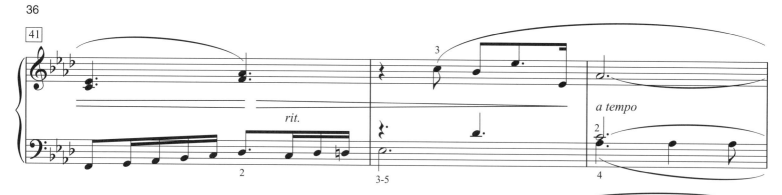

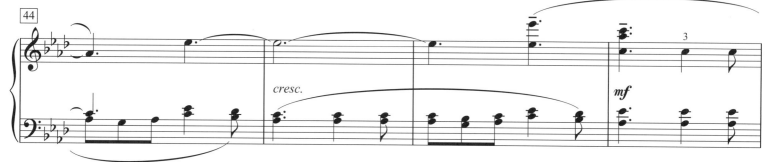

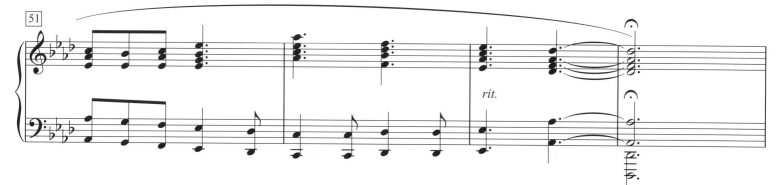

TIE YOUR MOTHER DOWN

Words and Music by
BRIAN MAY
Arranged by Phillip Keveren

Toccata (♩ = 144)

UNDER PRESSURE

Words and Music by FREDDIE MERCURY,
JOHN DEACON, BRIAN MAY,
ROGER TAYLOR and DAVID BOWIE
Arranged by Phillip Keveren

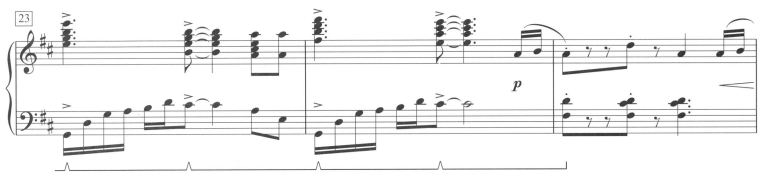

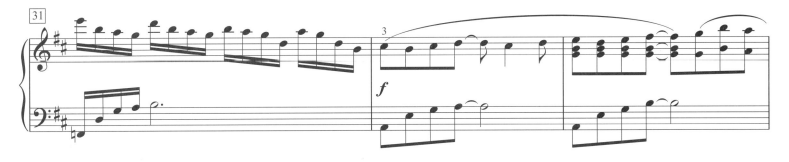

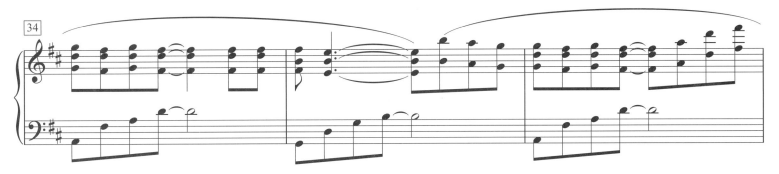

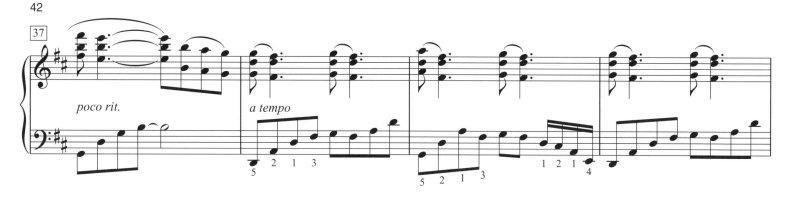

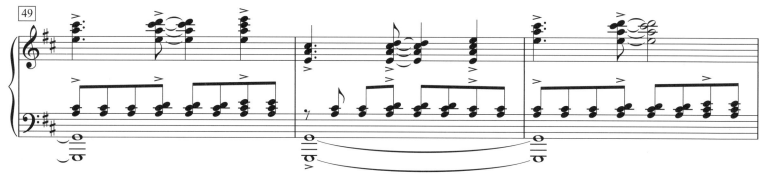

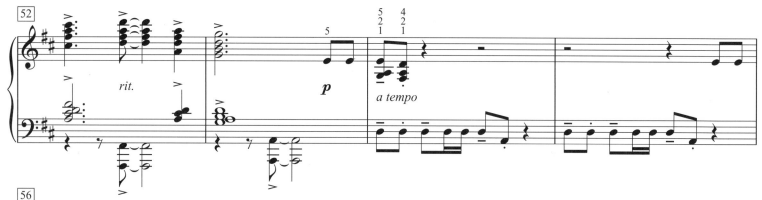

WE WILL ROCK YOU

Words and Music by
BRIAN MAY
Arranged by Phillip Keveren

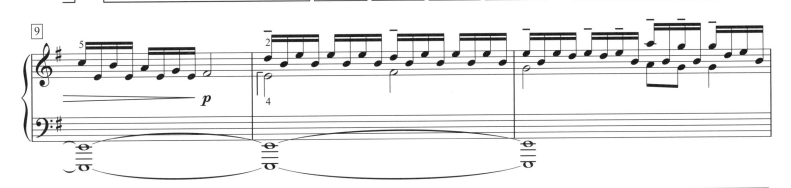

44

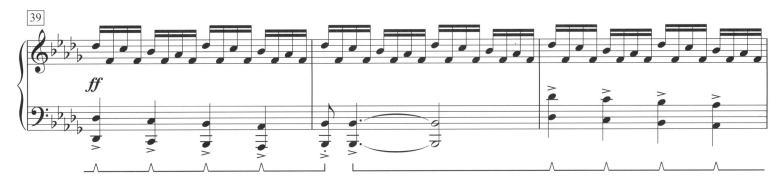

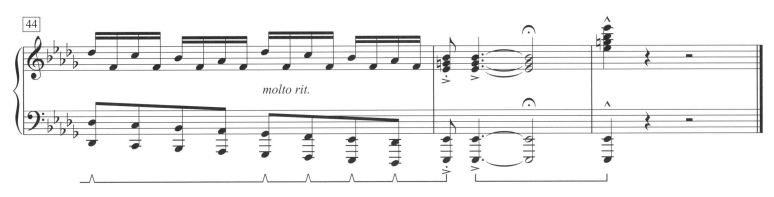

WE ARE THE CHAMPIONS

Words and Music by
FREDDIE MERCURY
Arranged by Phillip Keveren

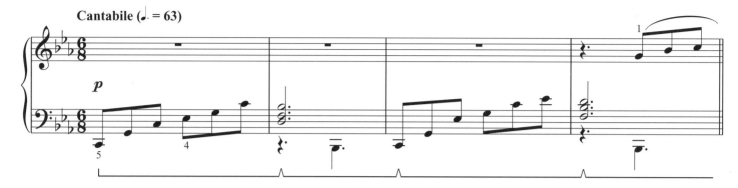

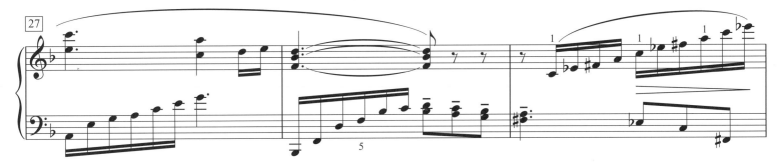

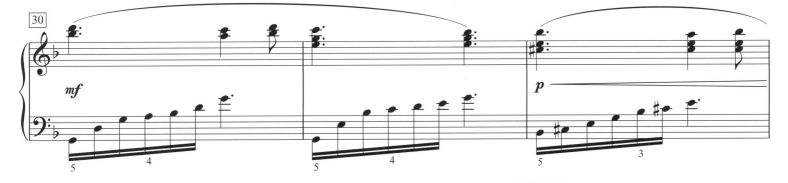

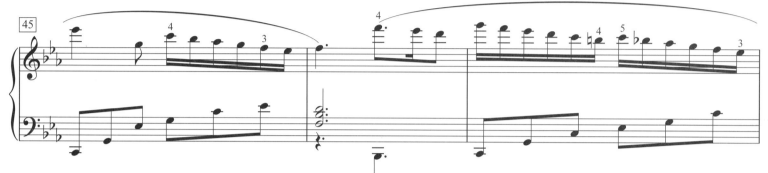

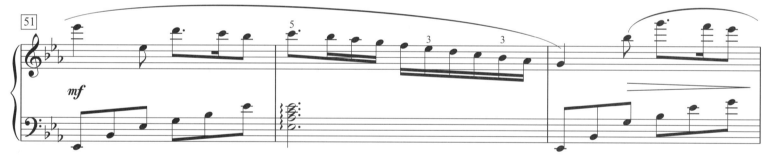

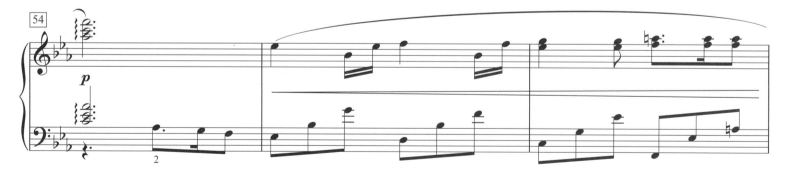

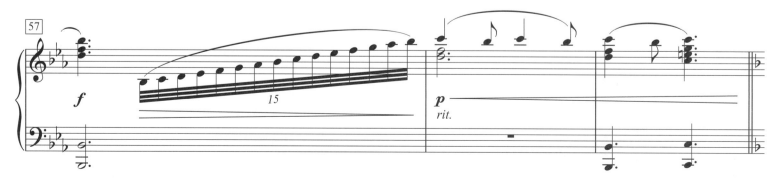

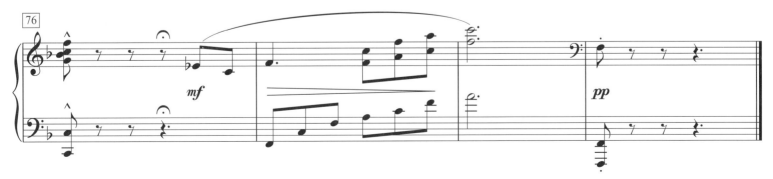

WHO WANTS TO LIVE FOREVER

Words and Music by
BRIAN MAY
Arranged by Phillip Keveren

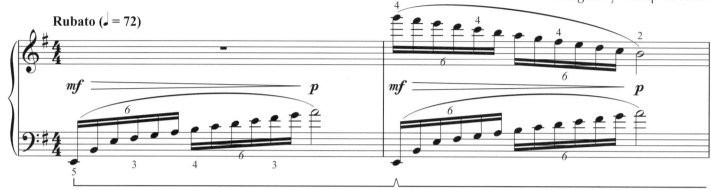

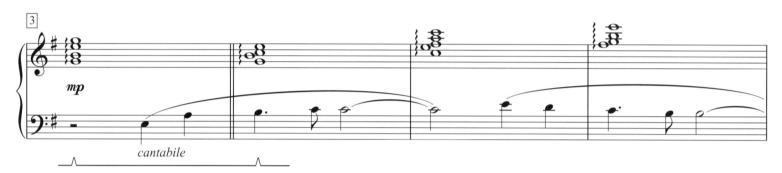

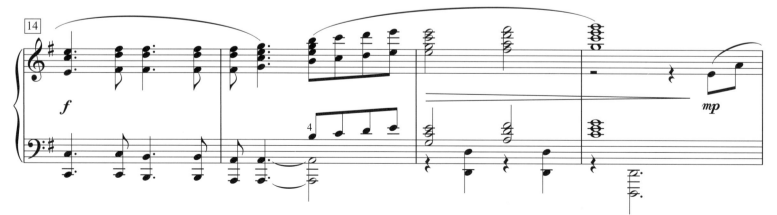

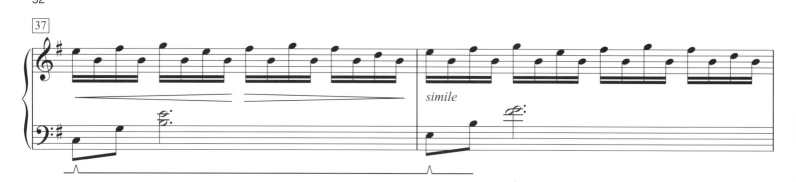

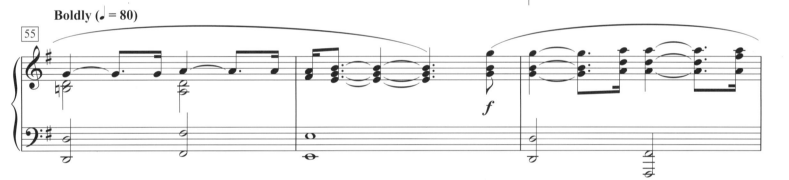

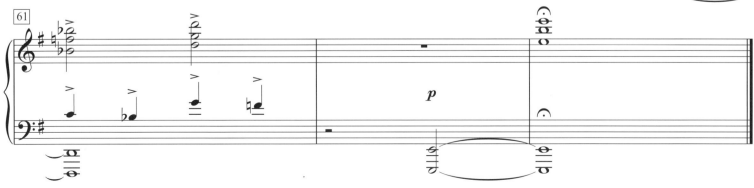

YOU'RE MY BEST FRIEND

Words and Music by
JOHN DEACON
Arranged by Phillip Keveren

Light-hearted (♩ = 126)

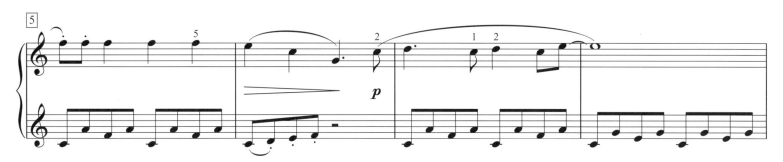

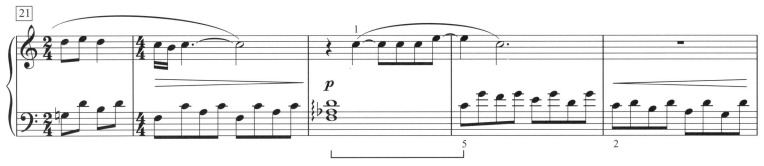

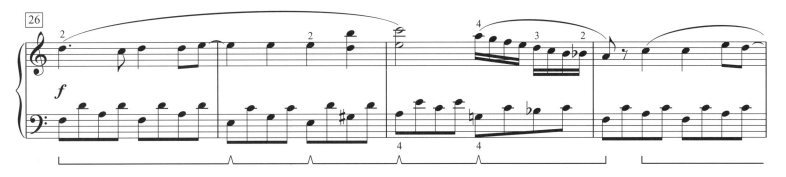

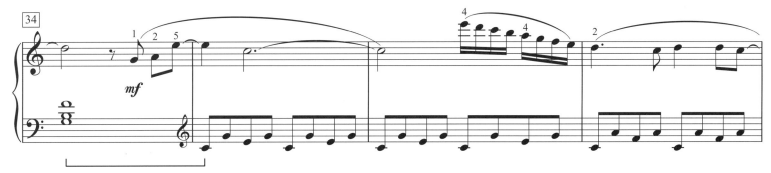

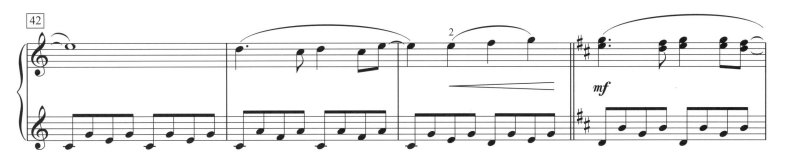

56